Creative Costumes

FOR ANY OCCASION

Mark Walker

First printing: October, 1984
Second printing: August, 1986
Third printing: October, 1987
Fourth printing: July, 1988
Fifth printing: December, 1989
Sixth printing: June, 1991
Seventh printing: June, 1992
Eighth printing: August, 1992

©Mark Walker, 1984

COOL HAND Communications, Inc.
A Publishing Company

All Rights Reserved. This publication may not be reproduced in whole or in part by any means without prior written consent.

Published by:

COOL HAND Communications, Inc.
1098 NW Boca Raton Blvd., Suite 1
Boca Raton, FL 33432

"Where there is never a failure to communicate"

Library of Congress #84-80941
ISBN 1-56790-056-9

Manufactured USA

To my brother, Scott

Contents

Introduction

Almost every good costume, no matter how simple or elaborate, will require *some* preparation and expenditure.

The basic instructions for the costumes in this book involve elementary pinning, sewing, gluing and dying of fabrics. Most of these costumes can be made with ordinary clothing articles found in the home. If you cannot locate a particular item, check with family members or friends, or purchase the garment through a second-hand clothing store. Frequently, these stores offer a wide selection of good merchandise at a reasonable cost. A list of these establishments can, of course, be found in your local telephone directory.

Many times a hat will convey the entire premise of the costume. Prop pieces such as clubs and canes can also add a delightful touch. Inexpensive hats, props, and accessory items are often sold at novelty and costume shops. Again, check your local telephone directory. Also, for your convenience, a few suppliers are listed in the back of this book.

The pages that follow offer a wide selection of costumes or costume ideas. Many will appeal to just about everyone. The amount of time and effort creating your costume will be amply rewarded when someone asks, "Where did you get that costume?" and you reply, "I made it myself."

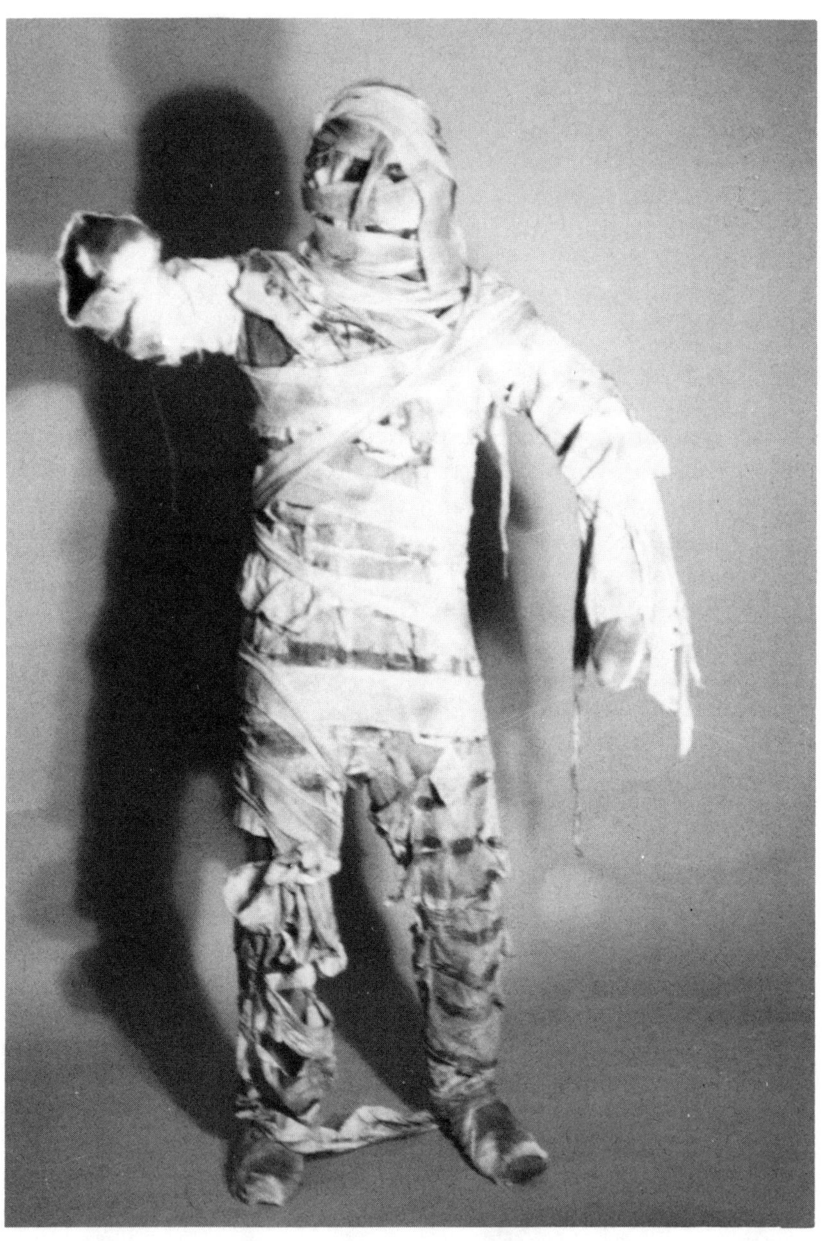

Mummy

Materials needed:

long johns
shoes
2½ - 3 inch wide strips of white fabric
white glue

Directions:

Tint an old white sheet or white tablecloth with a tan or brown fabric dye, or a concentrated solution of coffee or tea. Tear the material into strips approximately 2½ - 3 inches wide. Glue the strips together end to end forming very long strips. The strips will later be wrapped and glued to the long johns.

After you have put the long johns on, have someone wrap the long strips of fabric around your body as seen in the photograph. Tack the strips at various spots with white glue. To add some color, the costume may be sprayed with a brown color hair spray.

Rag Dolls

Materials needed:

- denim overalls
- white shirt
- funny hat
- white gloves
- black shoes
- cotton mops
- dress
- white apron
- knee-high socks
- blue fabric
- colored tape
- red fabric dye
- ribbon or elastic

Directions:

Roll up the pants legs of the overalls and hold them in position with rubber bands to give the appearance of knickers. If striped stockings are not available, stripe a regular pair of hose with colored tape.

Dye two cotton mops with red fabric dye and allow ample time for them to dry. The mop wigs can be held in place with a piece of elastic or ribbon.

With the blue material make a big bow for the gentleman and a bow for the lady's mop wig. Using red make-up color in the noses of the characters and with a black eyebrow pencil draw in the eyes and smiles.

Tropical Natives

Materials needed:

pieces of brightly flowered material
bathing suits
real or artificial flowers
leis
safety pins

Directions:

Secure one edge of the material to the bathing suits with safety pins and wrap and pin the material as shown on the models. A flower can be added to the young lady's hair and the leis can be worn around the neck. If leis are not available from your local novelty or costume shop, you can easily make them by stringing real or artificial flowers on a piece of heavy thread. A substitute for flowers are crumbled balls of colored tissue paper.

Detective

Materials needed:

two matching baseball caps
overcoat
matching material
safety pins
suit or dark coat and pants
white shirt
necktie
pipe
magnifying glass
stickpin
dark shoes

Directions:

Put on the shirt and turn the collar up as shown on the opposite page. Once the tie is in place, add the decorative stickpin.

A regular overcoat can be transformed into an inverness coat by adding a small cape cut from material similar to the coat. The cape can be held into position with safety pins.

As shown in the photograph, a deerstalker's cap is made by using two identical baseball caps.

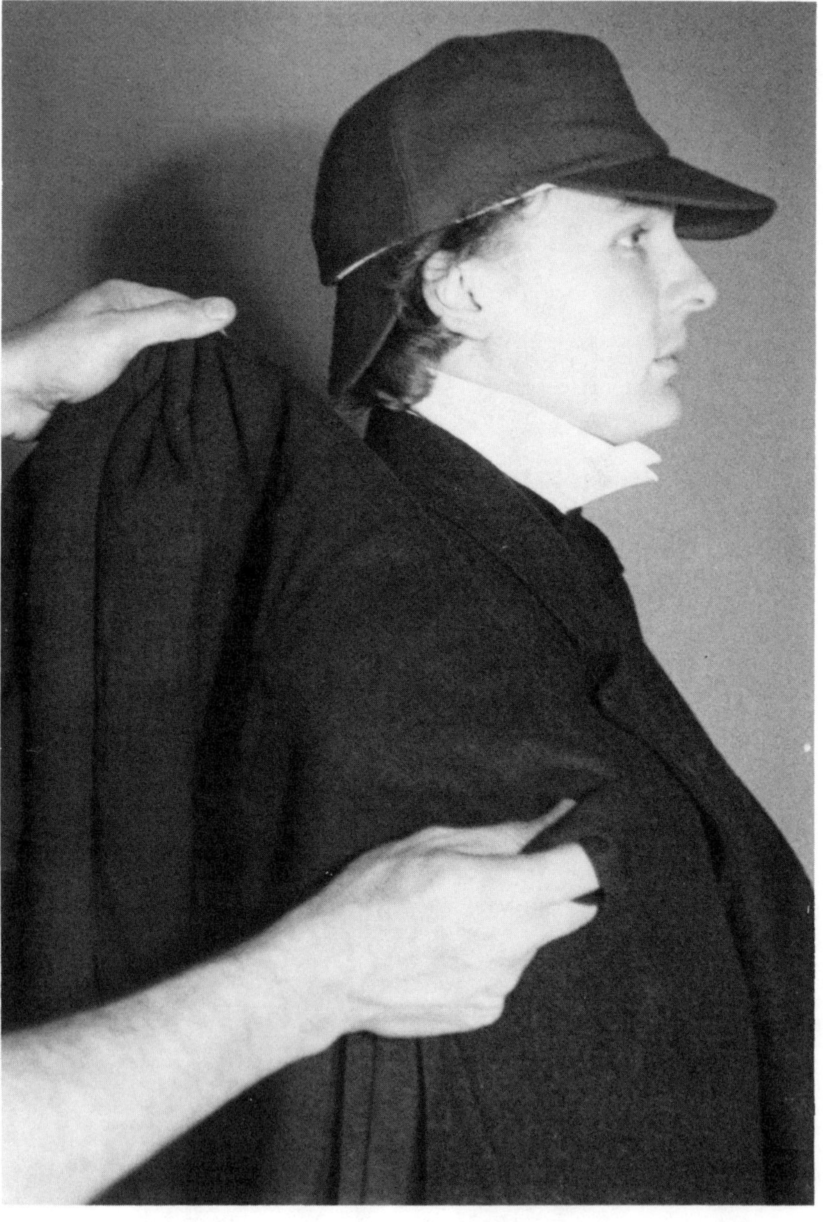

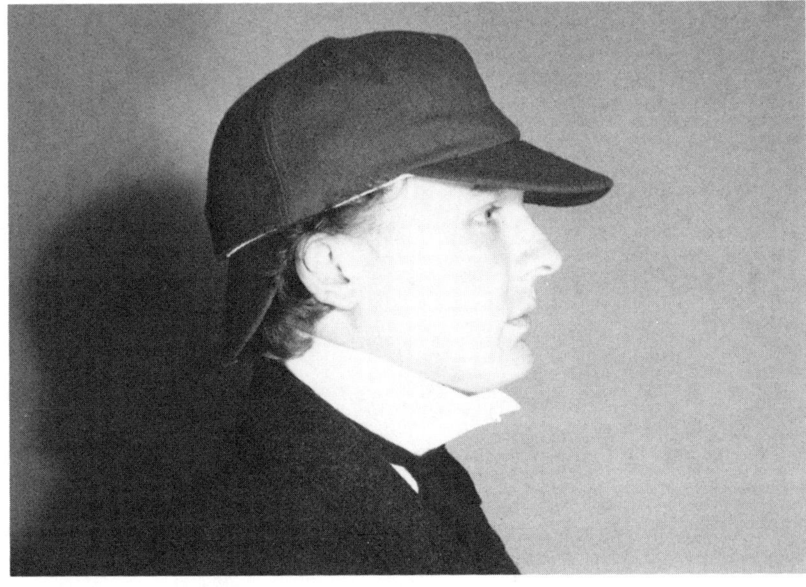

Harem Girl

Materials needed:

two-piece bathing suit
sheer material
assorted jewelry
slippers

Directions:

To make the skirt, take two pieces of sheer material and pin one to the front and back of the bathing suit. Add beads, pearls, small chains, and necklaces to trim around the waist of the skirt.

Pin or tack a piece of sheer material over the bra of the bathing suit. Once again, add decorative trim.

Attach a small locket or pendant to a length of sheer material and bobby pin to the hair as shown. Dangling earrings and a few bells add to the basic costume.

Pirate

Materials needed:

- full-sleeved white shirt
- pants
- kerchief
- sash
- earring
- eye patch
- sword

Directions:

The shirt should be opened at the neck and tied around the waist. Use a kerchief as a head scarf or make one out of a triangular piece of striped material.

The pants should be tattered at the bottom. Make a sash for the waist by using a bright piece of cloth 8 inches wide by 72 inches long.

A novelty sword, big earring, and eye patch complete the costume.

Absent-Minded Professor

Materials needed:

academic gown or choir robe	shirt
academic hat	tie
boxer shorts	garters or ¼ inch black elastic
socks	pair of glasses
dress shoes	text book

Directions:

The boxer shorts should have some type of design on them. If they are not available, simply draw and color in hearts or dots by using red magic marker.

Garters can be created by cutting several pieces of ¼ inch black elastic and with small safety pins they can be secured around the legs and to the socks.

The Piggyback Express

Materials needed:

mask and wig
blouse
skirt and underskirt
shawl
gloves
pants
boots or shoes
shirt
jacket
cardboard boxes
tape
safety pins
newspapers

Directions:

This costume will provoke more laughter than any costume you can imagine. The maximum expense involved would be that of a mask and wig.

Although it appears that there are two people in the picture, actually there is one person and one dummy. In this picture the rider is a man. The upper portion of his body is wearing a shirt and coat. The lower portion is wearing a skirt and underskirt.

The legs and boots shown in the photograph are in reality a pair of pants and boots stuffed with newspapers and pinned to the man's shirt under his coat. These legs are held in position by pinning them to the skirt. The boots are also pinned in place.

The upper torso of the old lady is merely a cardboard carton with newspapers stuffed on the outside to simulate the old lady's body. This is

covered with a long-sleeved blouse; shawl and stuffed gloves are pinned into position.

The mask is mounted on a styrofoam headblock which has been secured to the cardboard box. The old lady's torso can be held in place by securing the lower portion of the box around the waist of the rider with a cord or belt. The upper portion of the torso can be pinned to the shirt.

Shower

Materials ıeeded:

hoola hoop
shower curtain
bathing or swimming cap
shower brush
bathing suit
slippers
tape
rope
dowels
safety pins
string

Directions:

Attach two dowels to the hoola hoop with tape as illustrated. To hold the hoop in position, tie the hoop with rope as shown. Tie and/or pin the shower curtain to the hoop.

Little Boy and Little Girl

Materials needed:

long-sleeved shirt	short fluffy dress
pants	sash
suspenders	large hair bow
knee-high socks	white socks
cap	lollipop
lace shoes	black Mary-Jane type shoes
bandanna or kerchief	

Directions:

To make the costume for the little boy, remove the collar from a long-sleeved shirt. To give the appearance of knickers, roll up the pants legs and hold in place with rubber bands. Use make-up to add freckles and block out a tooth.

The girl's dress should be short to create the illusion of a little girl. If the dress is too long, simply pin it up. Use a piece of cloth 8 inches wide by 72 inches long to make a sash for the waist.

Foreign Legionnaire

Materials needed:

white shirt
white pants
white painter's hat
white cloth
black boots
toy pistol
2-inch white webbing

Directions:

Stitch or glue a piece of white cloth to the painter's hat as shown in the picture.

Measure the length of material you will need to go around the waist and over the shoulder. Use 2-inch white webbing if available. If the belting is not available, buy a roll of 2-inch white adhesive tape long enough for your requirements. As you unroll the adhesive tape, stick it on a piece of cloth. Then cut the strips using the tape as a guide. Fasten the belting in place with safety pins. A silver buckle can be made with cardboard and aluminum foil.

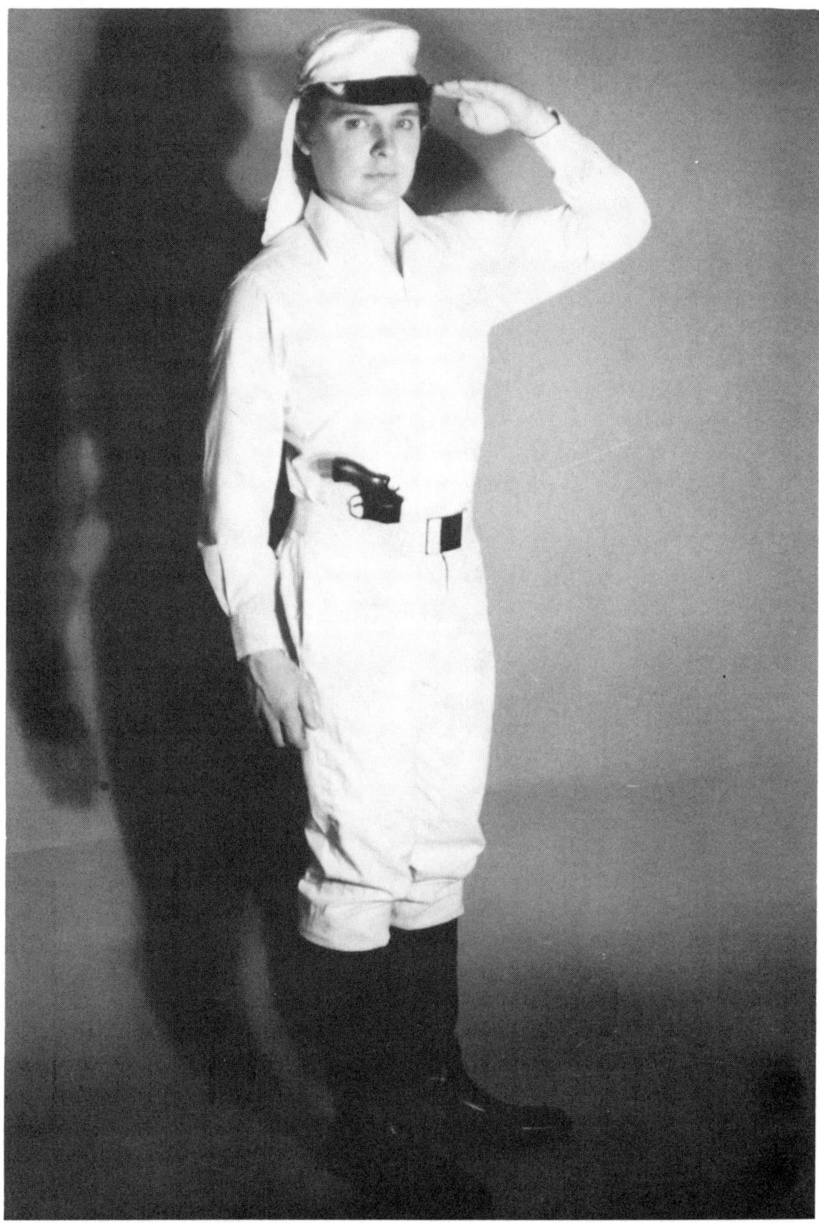

Prehistoric Couple

Materials needed:

bathing suits
old bathroom mats
burlap
pieces of fake fur
rope
old straggly wig
fake club

Directions:

The costumes for this Stone Age couple can be made out of a variety of materials such as old bathroom mats, burlap, pieces of fake fur, or any rough material. By draping and pinning the material you can achieve the effect as shown in the photograph. Pieces of rope or thin scraps of fur can be wrapped around the waist and wrists.

If you cannot locate a fake club, one can easily be made by following the directions explained in the *Club Sandwich* costume.

Money Bags

Materials needed:

several packages of fake money
staple gun or glue
safety pins
suit or overcoat
paper bags
magic marker

Directions:

Using a magic marker, draw a dollar symbol on each paper bag. To give the appearance of a filled bag of money, stuff a paper bag with newspapers. Next, either glue or staple the false currency so that it covers the newspapers and it overflows from the tops of the bags. Pin the paper bags—apparently filled with money—over an appropriate garment such as a suit or overcoat.

Laurel and Hardy

Materials needed:

light-colored suit
dark-colored coat and pants
derbies
white shirts
dark shoes
bow tie
regular necktie

Directions:

This popular comedy team wore various garments during their film career such as overalls, mismatched suits, etc. The most important part of the costumes are the derbies and ties. Also be certain to use black make-up to create a moustache for Ollie.

Bunny

Materials needed:

- one-piece bathing suit
- long-sleeved white shirt
- novelty rabbit ears
- dark nylons
- high-heeled shoes
- bow tie
- ball of cotton
- safety pins

Directions:

Cut off the collar and cuffs from the shirt and wear them as illustrated in the photograph. Bunny's tail can be made by pinning a large ball of cotton to the rear of the bathing suit. If you do not have a bow tie, make one out of cloth or paper and attach it to the collar.

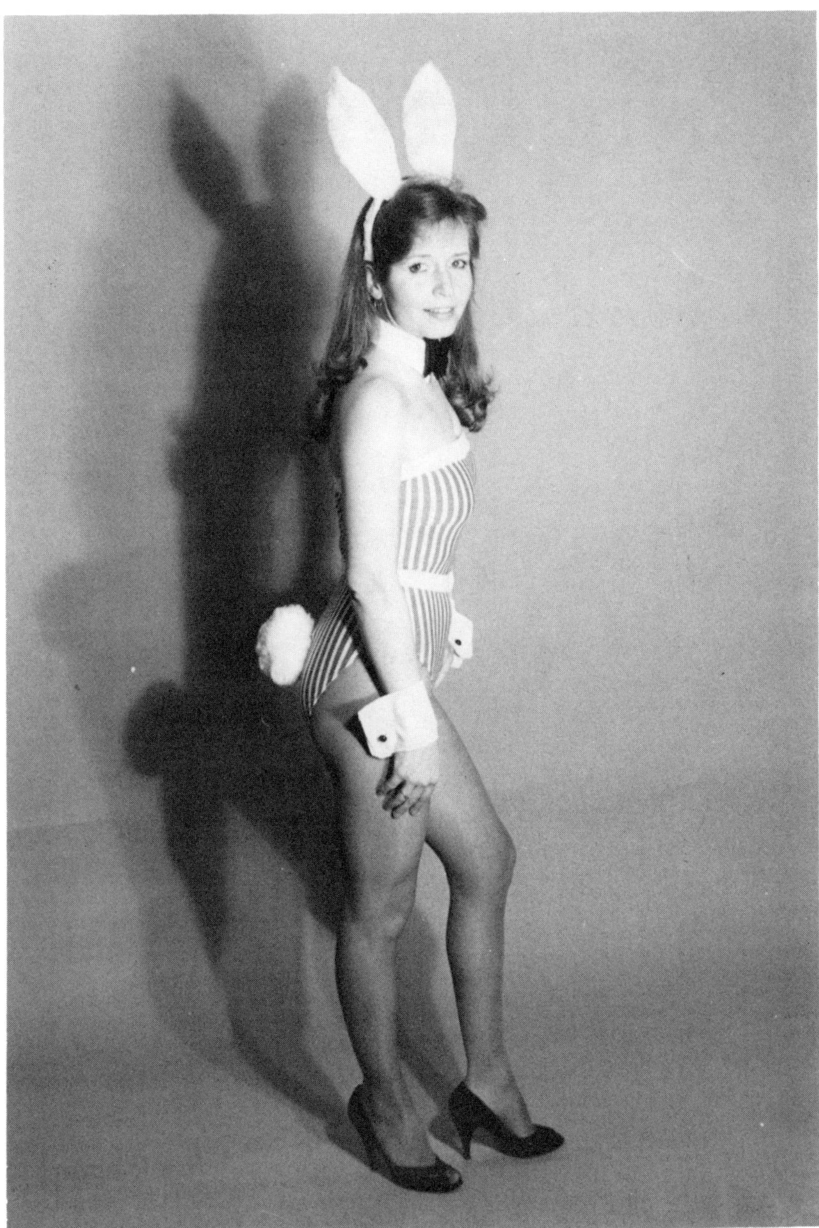

Greasers

Materials needed:

white undershirt	sweater set or blouse
straight leg dungaree pants	full skirt
black loafers	loafers
white socks	white tennis socks
	red ribbon
	felt or cardboard
	cotton
	chain or braid
	white glue
	jewel or button

Directions:

The man's costume is clearly illustrated by the photograph. Grease the hair and comb it straight back for a nice period touch.

The skirt should be a full skirt with crinolines or full petticoats. To make the poodle for the skirt, draw an outline of the dog on cardboard or felt. Cut out the silhouette of the poodle and form its body by gluing on cotton. Use the jewel to make the eye. The chain or piece of braid is used to make the leash and collar. Merely pin or tack the poodle in place.

High Roller

Materials needed:

- dark pants
- dark shirt
- red arm garters or rubber bands
- white tie
- white suspenders
- dark shoes
- white felt or cloth
- safety pins
- cigar

Directions:

This stereotypical character is associated with the pool sharks, hustlers, and tough guys of the 1920s.

Although there are no spats pictured, they can be made out of white felt or cloth and held in place with safety pins. Draw in fake buttons with a magic marker.

The hair should be slicked back and parted in the middle.

Civil War Soldier

Materials needed:

- gray or blue pants
- gray or blue kepi
- yellow ribbon
- suspenders
- boots
- long johns
- kerchief

Directions:

The color of the hat and pants will determine whether you are on the side of the north or south. Gray is for the Confederacy and blue is for the Union.

Pin, sew, or glue a piece of yellow ribbon on both sides of the pants. The real added touch is the kepi which is readily available from any novelty or costume shop.

Clown

Materials needed:

leotard and tights
white or colored crepe paper
funny hat
masking tape
safety tape
rubber ball or novelty clown nose

Directions:

The base for the clown costume can be made from a leotard and tights or dyed long johns.

Cut a piece of crepe paper the full length of the package approximately 10 inches wide. Gather the paper to form a ruff for the neck that is about 14-16 inches long depending on the size of the neck. Use a strip of masking tape through the middle of the ruff to hold the pleats in place.

Cut two pieces of paper the full length of the package approximately six inches wide to form ruffs for the wrists. Follow the same procedure used for the neck ruff.

Two-inch wide strips of crepe paper can be gathered on a safety pin to form pompoms for the shoes.

Obtain a clown nose from a local costume shop or make one from a hollow rubber ball and hold in place with a piece of elastic. Apply appropriate clown make-up.

Playing Cards

Materials needed:

- deck of playing cards
- everyday clothes
- sheets of large cardboard
- red and white paint
- kazoos or small novelty musical instruments
- headbands
- cloth tape or string

Directions:

To produce the giant cards, paint pieces of cardboard white; with red paint color in the pips of the cards. The cards can be held in place with cloth tape or string. A crown of cards can be made merely by placing the cards inside a headband.

Half Man, Half Woman

Materials needed:

- blouse
- skirt
- nylons
- earring
- lady's shoes
- man's pair of pants
- shirt
- jacket
- belt
- tie
- socks
- man's shoes

Directions:

To achieve the effect as pictured, put on each garment and mark and divide it in half. By cutting, sewing, gluing or stapling, join the various components. For a novelty touch, add appropriate make-up to each side of the face.

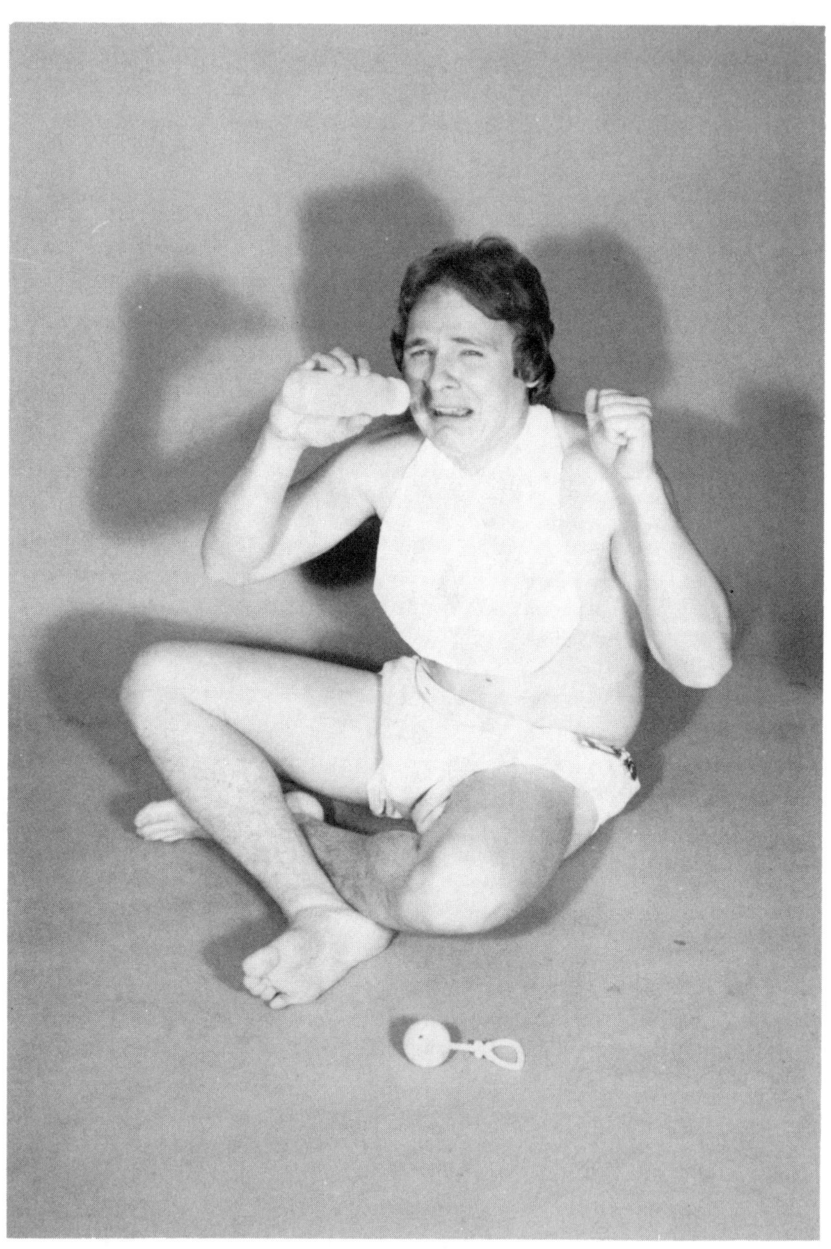

Big Baby

Materials needed:

two large pieces of white cloth
terry cloth towel
talcum powder
large safety pins
rattle
bottle

Directions:

A bib, cut from a terry cloth towel, may be pinned around the neck. Talcum powder should be sprinkled freely over the body not so much for a sight gag, but for the ever-present fragrance associated with a baby.

Stacked Deck

Materials needed:

bathing suit (one-piece or a bikini)
deck of playing cards
safety pins
adhesive tape
wire

Directions:

Using adhesive tape, attach the safety pins to the back of the playing cards. Having done this it is a simple matter to attach the cards to the bathing suit without harming the garment.

Tape several playing cards to a piece of wire, and pin the tiara-style headpiece into place with safety pins. Cards may also be attached to earrings for an additional touch. For some real fun, announce that you are a "stacked deck" or ask someone to "pick a card, any card."

Greek Couple

Materials needed:

- white sheets
- sandals
- laurel wreaths
- ropes
- safety pins

Directions:

Using sheets or pieces of material, wrap the bodies as shown on the opposite page. Secure the cloths in position with safety pins making sure that the pins are concealed in the folds of the cloths. Ropes or pieces of cloth, wrapped around the bodies, will add more interest to the costumes.

Laurel wreaths may be made from fresh or artificial leaves.

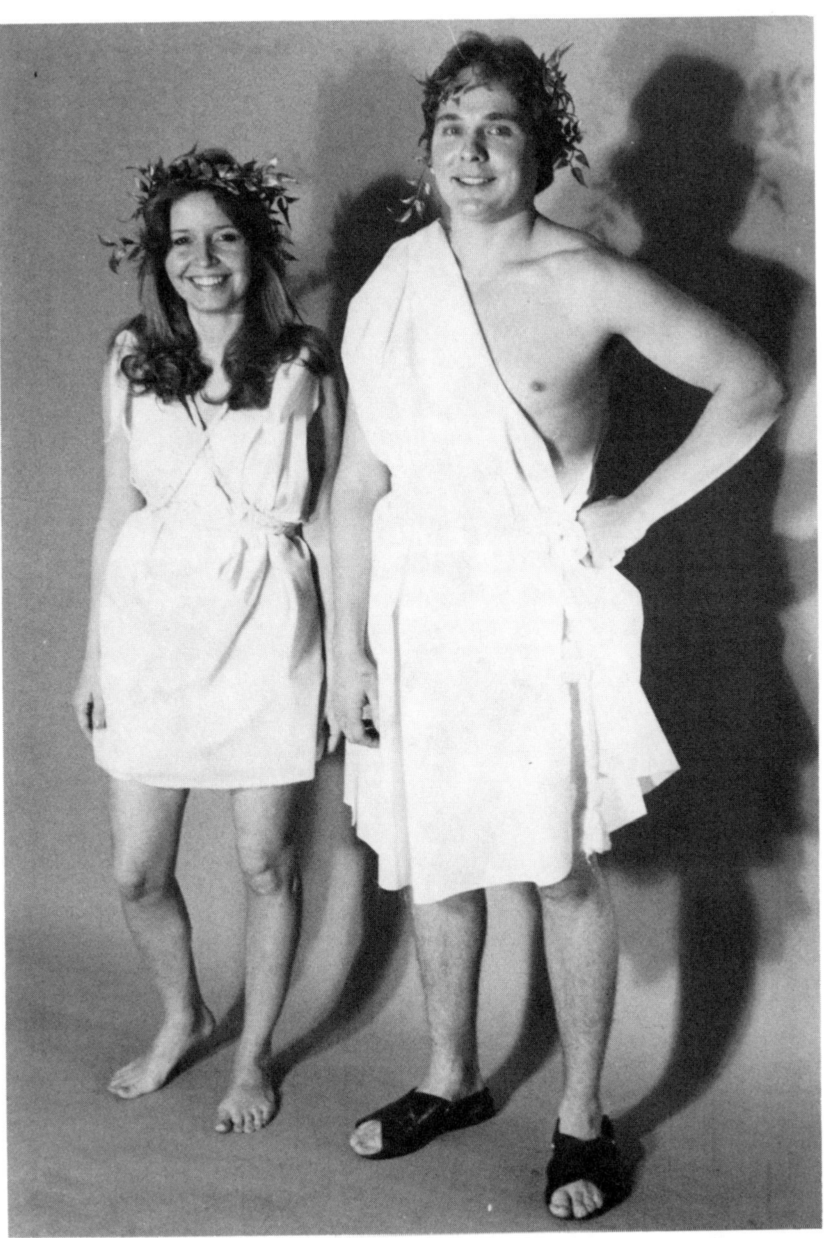

Space Travelers

Materials needed:

- black pants
- rain, ski, or work boots
- jersey, V-neck, or turtleneck sweater
- leotard and tights
- high-heeled shoes
- aluminum foil

Directions:

A basic space costume can be made from many things such as ski clothes, leotard and tights, sweaters, etc.

The headbands, wristbands, belts, and the space medallions can be made by cutting strips of vinyl, cloth, or foil. Let the design of your space medallion be limited only by your imagination.

Mysto-Chango

Although the effect of this costume is to change a person into an elephant, there are unlimited possibilities using this principle. This comedy costume requires considerable time and effort to make, sewing ability and two people to perform the illusion.

It is not the author's intent to go into detail on the construction of this costume, but to show the effect as it appears to the audience.

The following pages will reveal how the effect is accomplished. This costume is sure to be a crowd-pleaser and a prize-winner.

- The young lady is holding a cloth banner. Directly in back of her is a young man wearing a cape which is tied over his shoulders and around his waist.

- The banner is lifted in front of the man completely blocking him from audience view.

- When the curtain is lowered, the man has changed into an elephant.

- Notice that the performer is facing the audience and the elephant costume is on the backside of the cape.

- As the performer is blocked from the audience's view, he turns around and pulls the cape over his head.

- The performer is now in his set position before the curtain is lowered.
- Mysto-Chango—the transformation as it appears to the audience. Remember, by changing the backside of the cape there are unlimited possibilities.

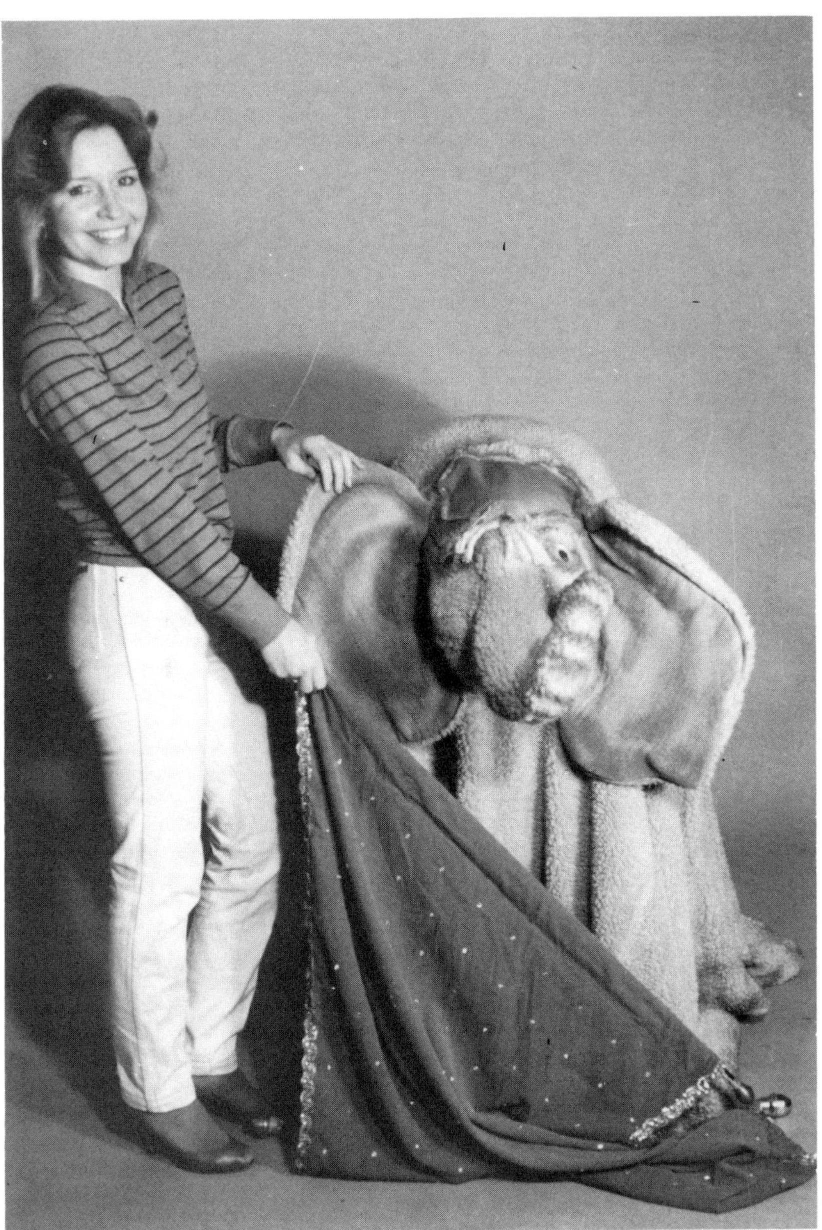

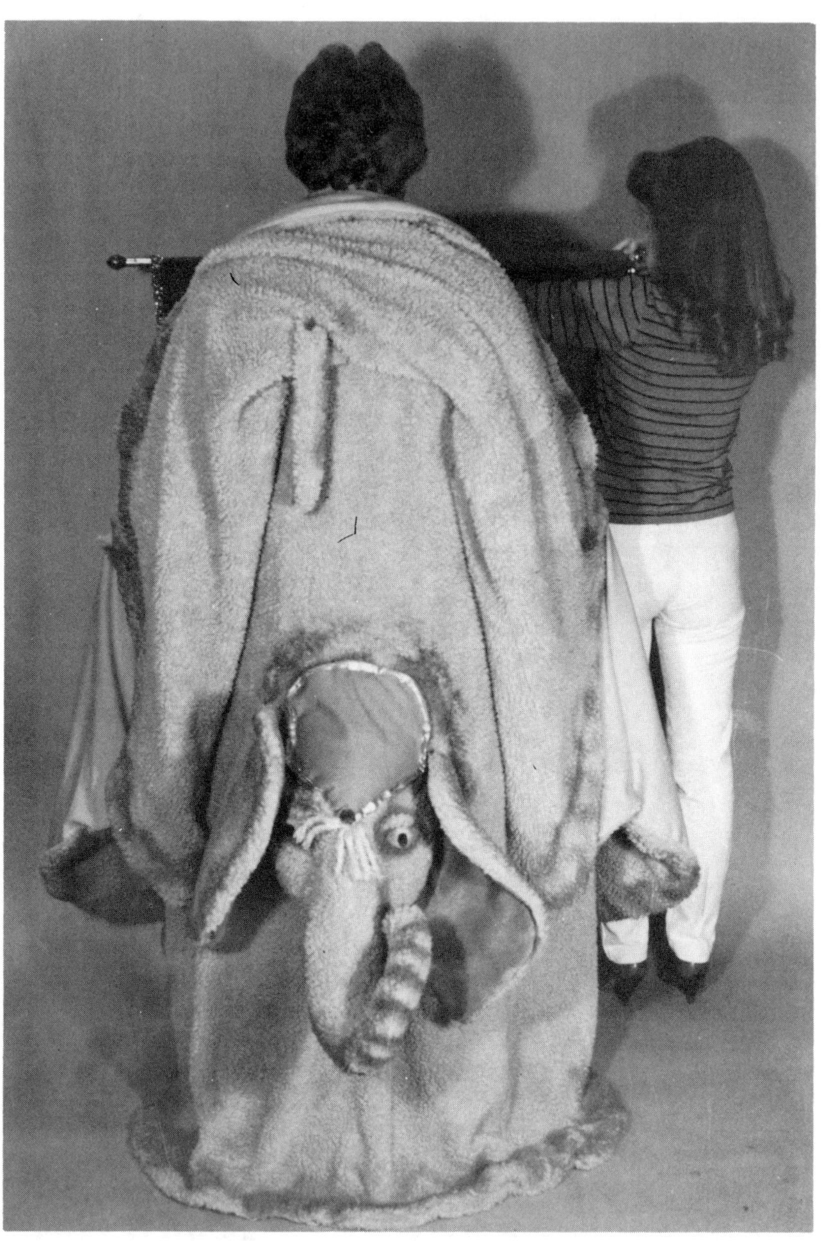

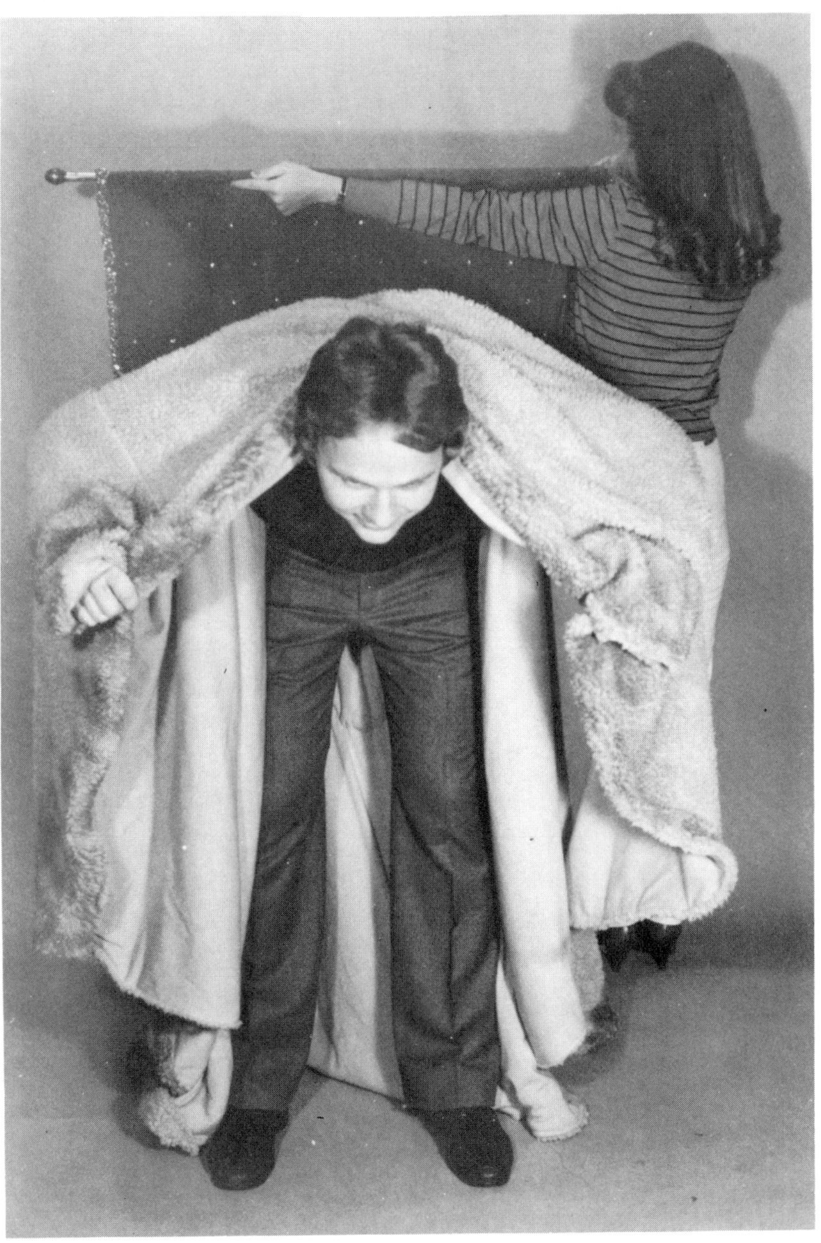

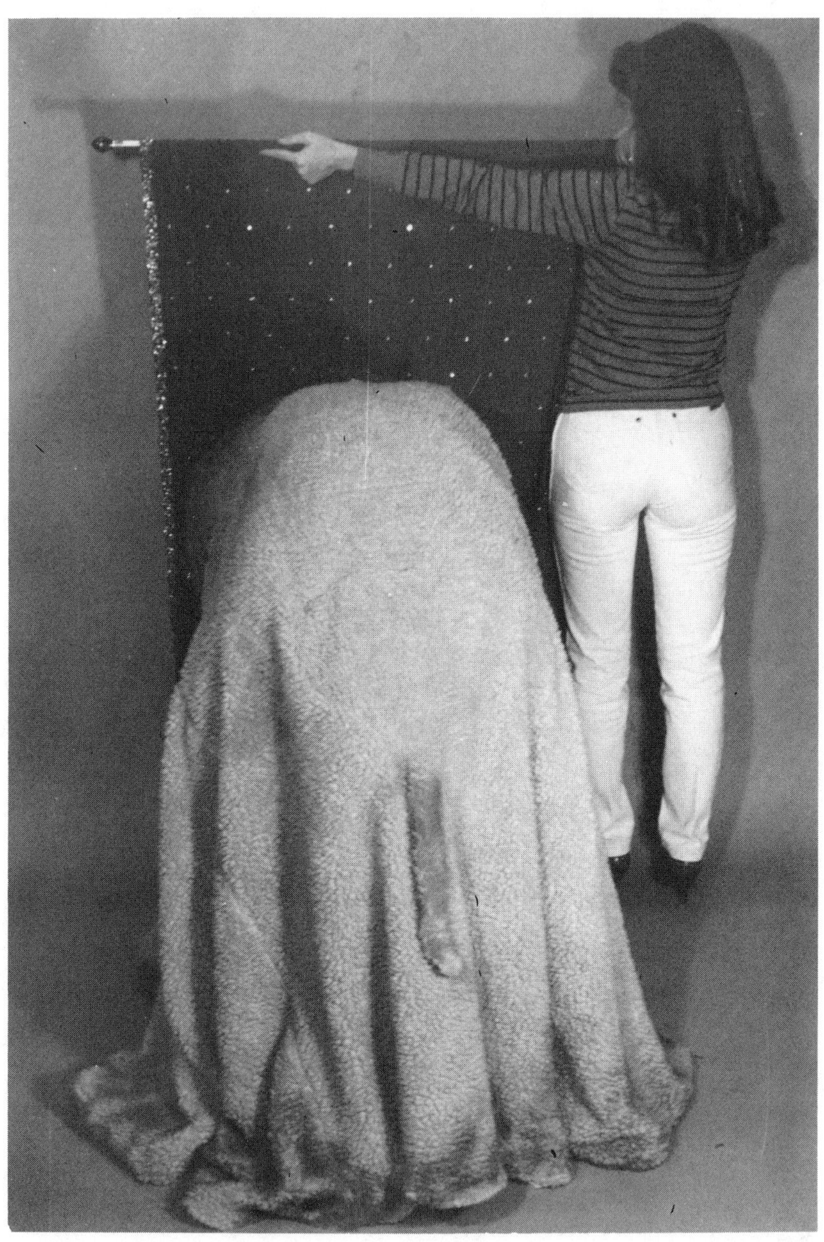

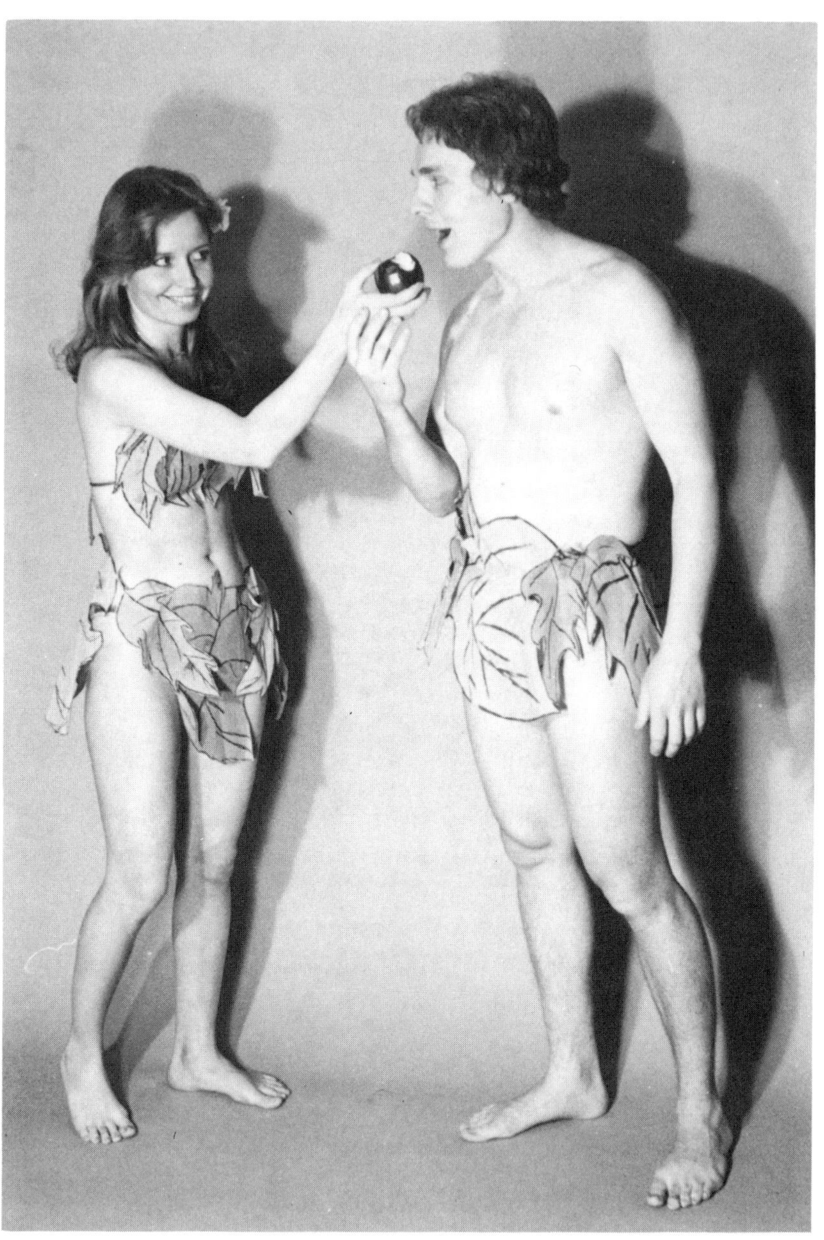

Adam and Eve

Materials needed:

- bathing suits
- green crepe paper
- safety pins
- black magic marker
- apple

Directions:

Cut out various-sized leaves from the green crepe paper and shadow them with a black magic marker. To secure them to the bathing suits, attach a safety pin to the back of each leaf. Pin the leaves at strategic points to the bathing suits.

Scarecrow

Materials needed:

- coat, pajama top, or smock
- baggy pants
- colorful shirt
- work gloves
- old hat
- sheer material
- old shoes
- burlap potato sacks
- six bright-colored patches
- magic marker
- straw
- pieces of rope

Directions:

Most of the items needed for this costume are explained by the photograph. Old shoes can be worn or burlap potato sacks can be wrapped around the shoes and secured with pieces of rope.

A square of sheer material should be cut large enough to fit over the head, gathered around the neck with a piece of rope and extend about six to eight inches below the rope. With a magic marker outline the design for the eyes, nose, and mouth.

The straw can be either stitched or pinned onto the costume.

Die

Materials needed:

cardboard box
white latex paint
black paint
paint roller
paintbrush
visor
leotard and tights

Directions:

Obtain a square box or one that can be cut to the shape of a die. Three holes will have to be cut in the box to accommodate the head and both arms. Make the holes equal in diameter.

Using white latex paint and a roller, paint the box. After the paint has thoroughly dried, use black paint to paint the other spots the same size as the three cut-out holes.

Wear a leotard and tights, dyed long johns, or a shirt and pants as undergarments.

Wonderful costumes can be created from boxes. Consult the *Great Halloween Book* for more box costume ideas.

Mexican

Materials needed:

- white long-sleeved shirt
- dark-colored pants
- sandals
- straw hat
- sash
- serape

Directions:

Wear the pieces of the costume as illustrated. Use a bright piece of cloth 8 inches wide by 72 inches long to make a sash for the waist. A serape can be created by wearing any brightly striped piece of material over the shoulders.

Use a black or brown eyebrow pencil to make a moustache.

Burglar

Materials needed:

- horizontally striped undershirt
- dark pants
- jacket
- cap
- dark shoes
- cloth mask
- suspenders
- carrying bag
- flashlight
- crowbar

Directions:

Wear the pieces of the costume as shown in the photograph. If you do not have a striped undershirt, use a plain white undershirt, a magic marker, and ruler to create one.

Apply a light coat of black make-up to the face to create a stubbly beard.

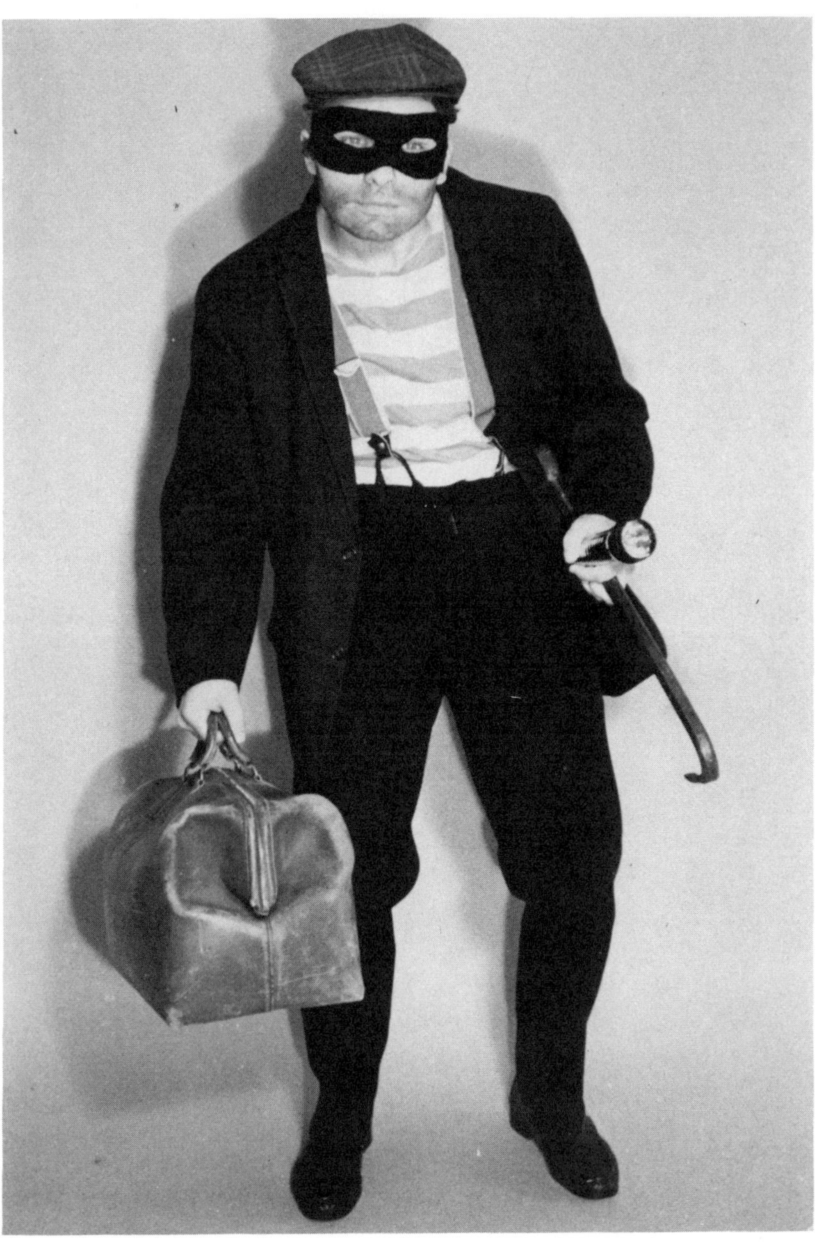

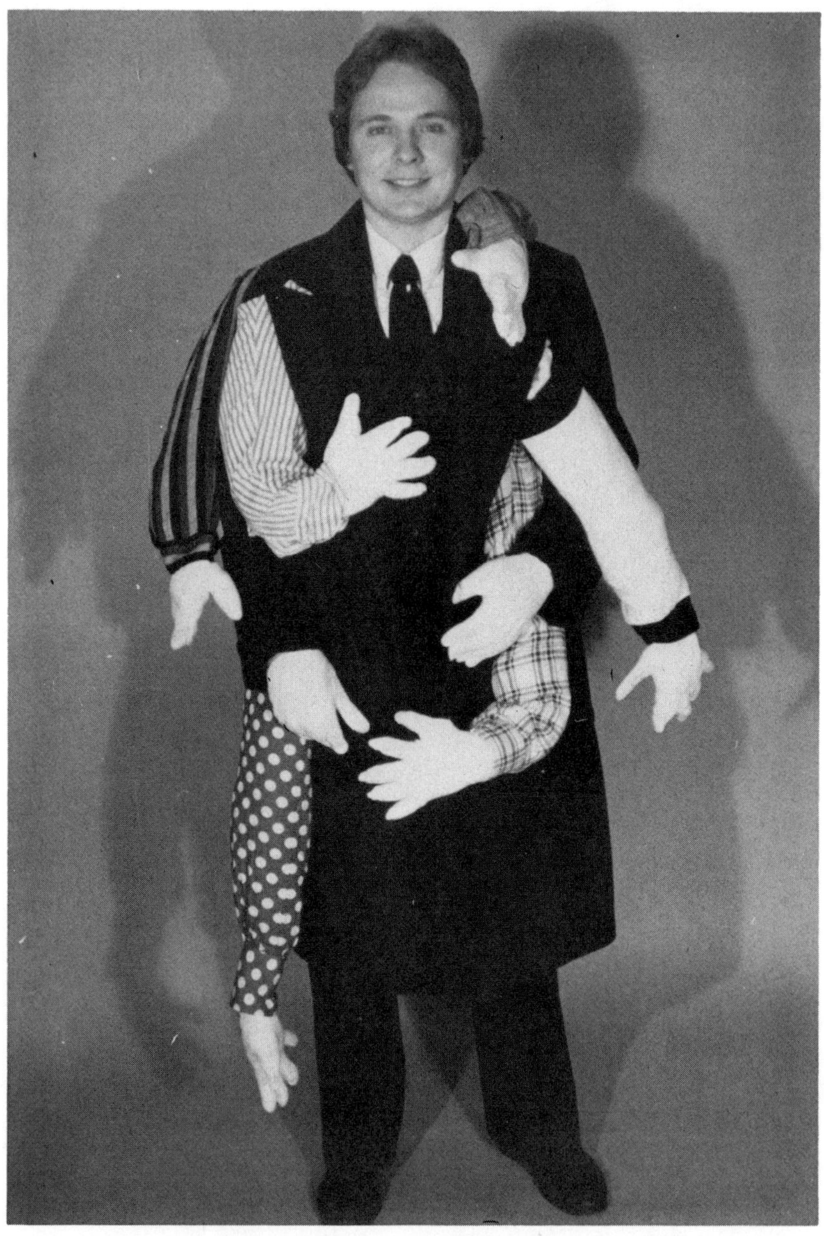

Coat Of Arms

Materials needed:

- overcoat
- shirt sleeves
- gloves
- safety pins

Directions:

Stuff the shirt sleeves with either cloth or newspaper and pin the sleeves to the outside of the coat. The gloves may be stuffed in the same manner and may be either pinned or sewed to the cuffs of the sleeves.

Shorty

Materials needed:

- knee pads
- cape or overcoat
- loafers or low quarter shoes
- full pants
- everyday clothes

Directions:

The most essential part of this costume is some sort of padding for the knees, so that you will be able to move about and not injure your legs.

To make it appear as though one has extraordinarily short legs, the pant's legs must be rolled up just below the knees. Bend in the back of a pair of loafers or low quarter shoes, put on the knee pads, and while kneeling, tape or tie the shoes just below the knees.

Be sure that the coat or cape covers the lower part of the legs that are bent back.

Club Sandwich

Materials needed:

two pieces of foam rubber
white shirt and pants
chef's hat
white and green crepe paper
fabric dyes
glue, staples, and tape
cardboard
chicken wire
brown paper
brown and black paint
magic markers

Directions:

Using a piece of bread as a guide, duplicate its shape on two pieces of foam rubber so that their size is proportionate to the body as seen in the photograph. Although you can cut foam rubber with scissors, you get a smoother finish using a sharp knife.

Use the excess foam rubber to make a piece of tomato and swiss cheese. To color the foam rubber tomato, cheese, and edges of the bread, use the fabric dyes. For the tomato and cheese, mix up a batch of dye and allow the items to absorb the color. Squeeze all the liquid out and allow them to dry. Use a magic marker to draw in the details. To color the edge of the bread, either use a paint brush or a cloth dipped in the proper color and coat the outer edge of the bread. The lettuce can be made out of green crepe paper.

(cont.)

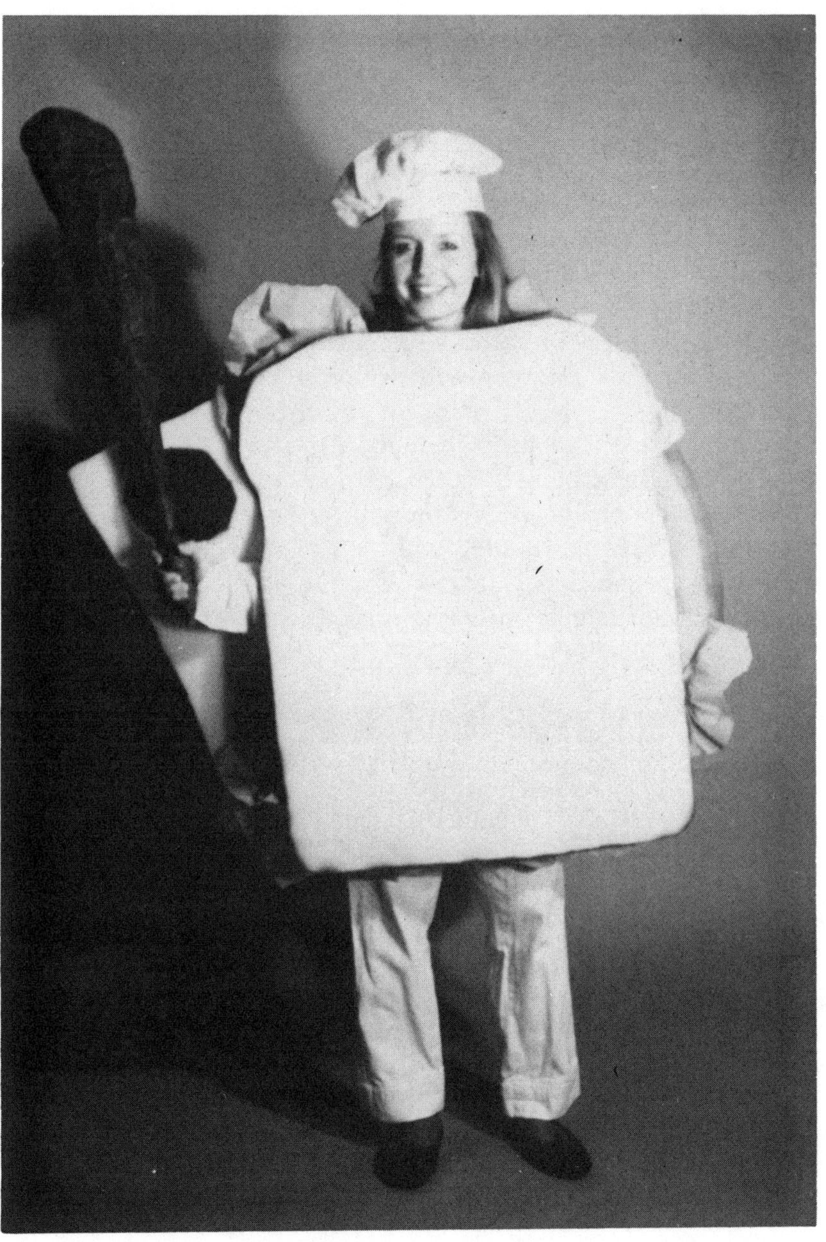

To attach the ingredients of the sandwich, use a contact cement. To hold the two pieces of bread in position, attach two strips of foam rubber to the front and back slices of the sandwich so that they rest on your shoulder. Two additional pieces of foam rubber may be glued or fastened to the lower corners on the inside of the sandwich. This will keep these pieces from separating.

If a chef's hat is not obtainable, one can be made by rolling a piece of cardboard into a tube to fit over the head. Cover the tube with white crepe paper by using glue or staples. The top of the chef's hat can be made from plain white crepe paper.

The club is fashioned out of chicken wire and covered with brown paper and entirely coated with white glue. The white glue will tend to soften the brown paper so that it takes the shape of the chicken wire. Allow the glue to dry and color the club with brown and black paint.

Bunch of Grapes

Materials needed:

- long johns or pajamas
- blue fabric dye
- blue 9-inch balloons
- artificial foliage
- green crepe paper
- safety pins
- slippers
- string
- tape

Directions:

Dye the long johns or pajamas blue. Attach safety pins at even intervals all over the blue costume. Inflate the balloons and tie pieces of string around their stems. To attach the balloons to the costume, thread the strings through the safety pins and tie them.

Head and legs pieces can be made from green artificial foliage readily available from any department store. The large leaf can be cut from green crepe paper and attached to the costume with tape and safety pins.

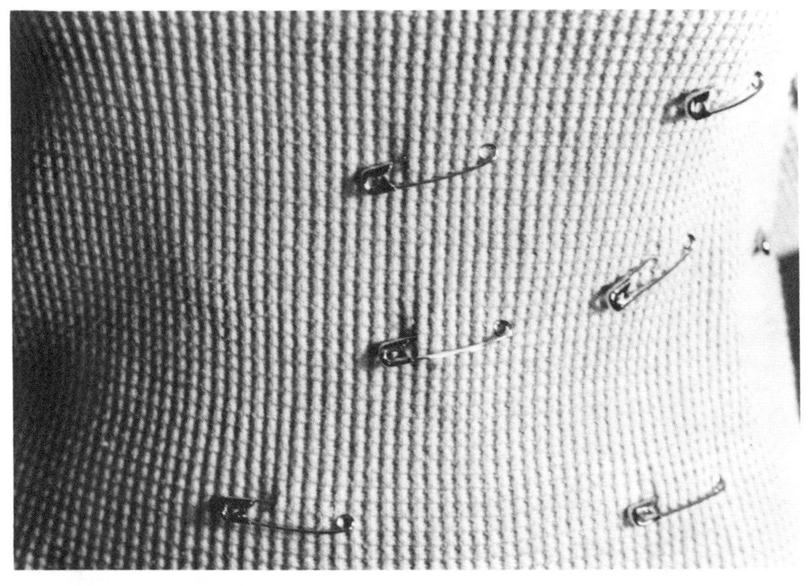

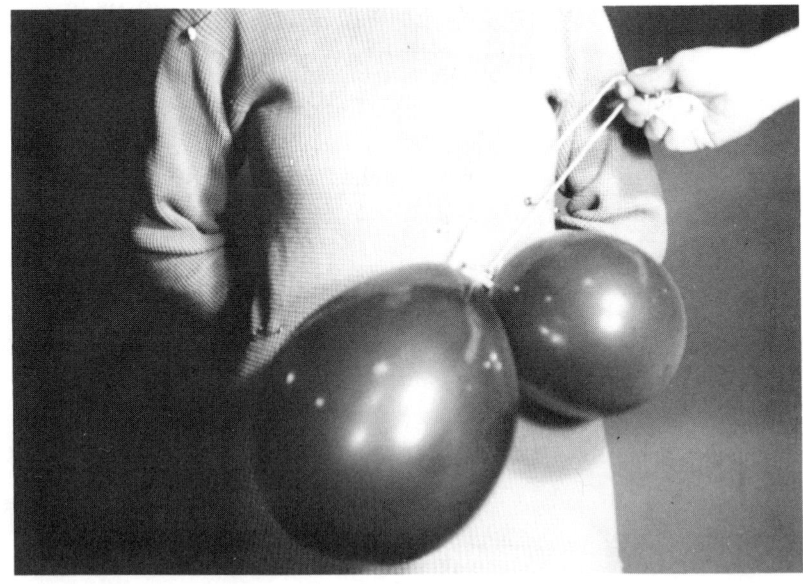

Tips and Suggestions

The following list of tips and suggestions should prove helpful in creating a costume:

- Metallic items such as buckles for belts and shoes, headbands, wristbands, or weapons can be constructed from cardboard and covered with aluminum foil.
- Foam rubber is easily accessible in different thicknesses. Use a sharp knife to get a clean cut. Two pieces of foam rubber can be held together with contact cement. Foam rubber can be used for props, novelty hats, accessories and major parts of the costume. It can be dyed with fabric dye, painted with spray paint, or colored with a magic marker.
- In many cases sewing can be avoided by using safety pins, glue, or tape.
- Imitation boot tops can be made by first cutting a pattern from a piece of paper to get the proper size and shape of the boots desired. Using the pattern, cut out the boot tops from heavy black cloth or vinyl. They can be stitched, glued or stapled up the back. Wear the boot tops over a pair of black shoes and socks.
- Stripes may be applied to fabrics or items such as socks and shirts by using a magic

marker and a ruler, or colored adhesive tape. An additional method is to stripe the portion of the fabric not to be colored with masking tape, spray paint the exposed portion and then remove the tape.

- Fabric dyes are inexpensive and can be used in many ways to completely dye or color portions of the costume. if you want a temporary coloring, washable hair sprays will tint or color the material.
- Designs such as dots, stars, and so on, may be added to the costume by using colored magic markers. If you want the designs to be removable, cut them from contact paper.

More Creative Costumes

Alpine Mountain Climber

The following articles are necessary to make this costume: a felt hat with a feather, white shirt, red or green 36-inch piece of ribbon, a pair of wide suspenders, a pair of short pants, plain colored knee-high socks (preferably green or red), boots, and a coil of rope. Tie the piece of ribbon around the neck for a necktie. Put the coil of rope over the shoulder and away you go.

Angel

A white robe, gold rope, aluminum wire, and Christmas garland are the basics to making this outfit. Details are found in the *Great Halloween Book.*

Battle Of The Bulge

Obtain the largest and longest long-sleeved, skirted dress available from friends or a local second-hand clothing store. Newspapers, foam rubber, or used plastic garment bags can be used for the padding. If a pair of long johns are available as an undergarment, use them to support the padding.

An inexpensive wig may add to the fullness of the face. If some asks, "Why are you so fat?" the person should respond, "I'm the battle of the bulge." This same idea can be adapted by using an oversized suit for a gentleman.

Cheerleader

A sweater, a short full or pleated skirt, and a large letter cut from felt and pinned to the sweater are all that are necessary for the ever-popular cheerleader. Pompoms can be made by using strips of crepe paper taped to a wooden dowel.

Christmas

With a white academic robe and gold rope, fashion the dress for this guise after the *Angel* in the *Great Halloween Book.* You might want to spray your hair with red and/or gold hair glitter. Then place holly sprigs wherever you can on the robe. Tuck some underneath the rope, make a chain of sprigs to hang down the skirt, around the neck, or wear holly in the hair. Carry gold glitter in a little satchel and during the evening, sprinkle good tidings everywhere!

Christmas Present

A box covered with Christmas wrapping paper and decorated with ribbon makes for a fun and easy costume. Wear a red or green leotard underneath the box to effect the Christmasy look. Tape a gift card to the box for a more realistic touch.

Cloud

Cut two identical cloud shapes from sturdy cardboard. Paint both sides of each piece of cardboard with white paint. You may want to add some gray paint touches for cloud depth. For the shoulder straps, loop two pieces of string through the front and back clouds—one for the left and one for the right shoulder. A white beret or a tuft of cotton can be worn on the head. Wearing a silver leotard underneath, you can effect a "cloud with a silver lining." A "9" painted on the front and back clouds creates "cloud nine."

Country Bumpkin

The country bumpkin's clothes are generally ill-fitting. The basic problem is the clothes are too short and too tight. To make your own clothes gives this appearance, turn up the sleeves of the coat and the pants legs. They may be held in place with safety pins. Add to this a bright necktie, a pair of white socks, work-type boots and a straw hat. To fill out the overall appearance of this character, use an eyebrow pencil to make freckles for the face and obtain a set of novelty buck teeth.

Dorothy

Dorothy's ruby slippers can be made by coloring any pair of closed-toe, low-heeled shoes with red paint. After the paint dries, cover each shoe with glue and sprinkle with red glitter. A dress similar to the one in the *Little Girl* costume can be used. Ideally, the dress hem should be right below the knee. Put on short white socks and the ruby slippers. The hair should be worn in two braids with bows at each braid's end. A wicker basket with a stuffed toy dog inside punctuates the outfit.

Elf

Creating a fringed effect, cut one-half to one inch wide strips at the bottom of a long, oversized shirt. Each fringe should measure between six and eight inches in length, depending on the effect you want. To some or all of the strips, attach bells. (Bells can be found in any five and dime or arts and craft shop.) Paint an old pair of flat shoes green and either sew or glue a bell onto each shoe. Draw a circle on each cheek and color in with red make-up. To simulate long eyelashes, draw vertical lines on the eyelids and beneath each eye with an eyebrow pencil. Wear a red or green leotard and tights underneath the shirt. A matching cap is an excellent accessory.

Executioner

This is an easy costume to put together. The only clothing articles that are necessary are a pair of black pants and a pair of boots. Add to the aforementioned articles a hood and bare chest and the basic costume is complete. The hood is merely cut from two pieces of cloth either glued or sewed together with eyeholes cut out.

Use a broomstick to create the handle for a fake ax. The ax blade can be fashioned from cardboard and covered with aluminum foil for an added highlight.

French Artist

A beret, a smock, and a piece of material tied into the shape of a large bow tie are the main characteristics of a French artist. Cut a palette from a piece of cardboard, and dab on spots of different colored paints. Add a paintbrush and a small penciled-in moustache to make the image complete.

Gangster

The *Gangster* is fashioned in the same vein as the *High Roller.* A dark suit, shoes, dark shirt, white tie, and a fedora are needed to complete this outfit. More instruction is found in the *Great Halloween Book.*

Garbage Man

Fill a trash bag with newspaper to fill the bag out. Tie the bag loosely at the neck. Stuff colored paper halfway into the bag wherever possible to create an overflowing garbage effect. White paper could substitute for eggshells, green paper for lettuce, etc. If you choose to effect the look of a garbage can, top the costume off with an upside-down pie plate worn on the head like a garbage can lid.

Geisha Girl

Using clown white make-up, cover entire face except for lips. Outline the eyes with brown or black eyepencil. Color the lips with red lipstick. For the hair, wrap hair onto the top or back of head. Insert two thin plastic or painted, wooden 12 inch dowels. Don slippers and a silk or satin kimono-style robe. For realism, remember to remove your shoes upon entering someone's home.

Ghoul

The ghoul requires preparation time to apply make-up. Make-up application tips and pictures can be found in the *Great Halloween Book.*

Gladiator

Follow the costume instructions for the *Greek Couple.* The only addition is to carry a sword made from cardboard and aluminum foil.

Gypsy

Colorful clothing and jewelry are the basics to the *Gypsy.* Use the tips in the *Great Halloween Book* to create an exotic ensemble.

Indian Girl

A sexy Indian girl costume can be made by using a bikini bathing suit and brown fabric. Follow the same procedure as used in the *Harem Girl* costume. To form a loin cloth, cut two strips of material and pin one to the front and back of the bikini briefs. Cover the bra with the same material. Use a small strip of material, one-inch wide and long enough to be tied around the head, to make a headband. Other costume accessories include a feather for the headband, a long black wig, and proper make-up.

Insect

Cut holes for arms and legs out of a trash bag. Fill trash bag with newspaper. Wear a pair of antennae fashioned from wire clothes hangers. To create large insect eyes, use black make-up to draw a large circle around each eye and color the circles in. Wear brown tights and brown shoes. Spots made from paper and glued to the bag allow you to create all kinds of insects.

Invisible Man

For this disguise, you'll need a suit, shirt, tie, hat, dark sunglasses, dark shoes, white gloves, and a white cloth. Cut out holes for the eyes in the white cloth and wrap the cloth around head. Put on the remaining clothing and voila! a simple, inexpensive costume.

Jack-In-The-Box

This unique box costume is created with a box, cord, paint, and fabric. Consult the *Great Halloween Book* for details on construction.

Lady Pirate

Almost any articles of clothing can be adapted for effecting this female counterpart to the *Pirate* costume. For ideas in assembling the *Lady Pirate* outfit, consult the *Great Halloween Book.*

Little Red Riding Hood

A fluffy dress, similar to the one in the *Little Girl* costume is used. Wear Mary Jane-style shoes with short, white socks. Carry a wicker basket of goodies.

Mime Artist

A white long-sleeved leotard, red suspenders, and a pair of dark pants are necessary for this costume. However, proper make-up is absolutely required to make this character complete. Consult your local costume shop for more details. A character novelty hat such as a derby or beret can also be added.

Movie Director

A beret, sunglasses, khaki pants, boots, sport coat, and a turtleneck sweater or a white scarf tied around the neck are the basic components for a movie director. A megaphone makes a wonderful hand prop.

Old Age

The materials you'll need to create the guise of an old man or woman are liquid latex, a sponge, powder puff, translucent powder, a baby brush or soft paint brush, brown or maroon eyebrow pencil, brown, grey or dark maroon make-up, silver/grey hair spray or liquid hair whitener, make-up remover, and a hair dryer. Pictures and further details to create this strikingly real illusion are found in the *Great Halloween Book.*

Pilgrim

Use a plain suit (preferably a dark color). Fold over the lapels and pin in place to give the appearance of a pilgrim's coat. Add a collar and cuffs cut from white cloth or paper. Either tack, sew or pin these articles in place. Turn up the pants legs to give the appearance of a pair of knickers holding them in place just below the knee with rubber bands. Long white socks or tights along with buckles for the shoes, made from cardboard and covered with aluminum foil, add the final touch to a pilgrim's costume.

Playboy

Using your best blazer-type coat, add a white scarf and a pair of sunglasses. A handkerchief in the breast coat pocket and a cigarette holder are the stereotypical touches associated with this character.

Prison Inmate

Using a black magic marker, put a five-digit number on the back of a denim or blue work shirt. The same number should be repeated on the front left side of the shirt. A pair of dark pants, work boots, and plastic chains around the wrists and ankles are all that are needed to give this costume an authentic look.

Robot

This is a simple box costume fashioned after the *Die* costume. The *Great Halloween Book* offers details on construction.

Russian Roulette

This guise is patterned after the *Big Baby* costume, yet, two additions are required. Wear a crown made from paper and aluminum foil marked with "CZAR" on the front. Carrying a toy water pistol completes this unique play on words.

Sheik

A white academic gown, a dark over-robe, a white cloth, and sunglasses are the essentials to making this outfit. Further instructions are found in the *Great Halloween Book.*

Spanish Señorita

To assemble a señorita's costume, use an off-the-shoulder white blouse, a piece of material long enough to make a sash for the waist, and a brightly colored full skirt with an underskirt. Make a mantilla out of a piece of lace and bobby pin into place with a rose on one side. Large hoop earrings, a shawl and a long stem rose held in the teeth are all that are needed.

Statue Of Liberty

Obtain a picture of the Statue of Liberty to use as a guide for making this costume. Drape a white sheet over the body (as seen in the *Greek Couple)* and tie it in place with a piece of white rope. The crown, torch, and tablet can be fashioned out of cardboard and glue. A stone-like finish can be given to the crown, torch, and tablet by using a stucco paint. A flashlight placed in the torch with a piece of red cellophane or crepe paper covering the lens will make a nice addition.

Television

This box costume is similar to the *Robot* and *Die*. For details, see the *Great Halloween Book.*

Turkey

This gag costume is similar in idea to the *Piggyback Express.* Consult the *Great Halloween Book* for instructions.

Upstairs Maid

Although this costume can be used in many ways, it could accompany a person wearing the *Playboy* costume. The upstairs maid can wear as many or as few of the following articles as she wishes: a sheer shorty pajama, a pair of dark pantyhose, a little frilly apron, a lace doily bobby pinned to the hair to make a maid's cap, a red garter around the leg, and a feather duster.

Witch

The results of creating this guise are well-worth the effort. Follow the basic instructions in the *Great Halloween Book* and then add your own personal touches for a unique costume.

Wizard

Glue cutouts of stars onto a dark-colored academic robe. Make a hat by forming a cone out of sturdy paper; glue. Cover the cone with material that matches the gown. Glue stars onto hat. Two effective additions are to wear a gray beard and to carry a magic wand. If you don't carry a wand, carry gold glitter as magic dust to sprinkle every once in a while.

Wolfman

The *Wolfman* requires a considerable amount of preparation, but like the *Witch,* the results are worth the time put forth. You'll need fangs, black and brown make-up, nose putty, a werewolf nose, werewolf ears, crepe hair, spirit gum, spirit gum remover, and make-up remover. See the *Great Halloween Book* for instructions for make-up application.

NOTES

SUPPLIERS

.T. JONES & SONS, INC.
08 N. Howard Street, Baltimore, Maryland 21201
301) 728-7087
lalloween Headquarters - suppliers of spider webs, horror masks and hands, make-up, books apes, props and numerous Halloween accessories. Enclose two first class stamps for brochure.

ORRIS COSTUMES
108 Monroe Road, Charlotte, North Carolina 28205
704)332-3304
lasks, novelty items, and assorted Halloween accessories.

UBIE'S COSTUME COMPANY
ne Rubie Plaza, Richmond Hill, New York 11418
718) 846-1008
umerous costume accessories and prop items available. Enclose $3.00 for catalogue.

TROBLITE COMPANY, INC.
30 West 14th Street, New York, New York 10014
212) 929-3778
uminous paint, ultraviolet paint and special theatrical lights ideal for haunted houses. Free atalogue available.

---

he Great Halloween Book and *Creative Costumes* are published by COOL HAND ommunications, Inc. Both books are available in better bookstores nationally, or may be rdered directly from the publisher. Mail a check or money order to COOL HAND ommunications, Inc. 1098 N.W. Boca Raton Blvd, Suite 1, Boca Raton, FL 33432.

---

entlemen:

Please rush the following order to the address noted below. Enclosed is my check for $__________ which includes the retail price of the title(s) noted plus $2.00 for shipping nd handling.

_______copies of *The Great Halloween Book* ($7.95 each)
_______copies of *Creative Costumes* ($6.95 each)

hip to:

Name______________________________
Address______________________________
City/State/Zip______________________________

Florida Residents: Please add 6% sales tax to the retail price of your order.

Acknowledgements

I would like to extend my sincere appreciation to the following individuals who helped make this book possible:

Models Yvonne Black and Scott Walker; photographer Emmy Molsion; and expert costumer George Goebel of the A.T. Jones and Sons Costumers. The costumes that appear in this book were especially created for this publication under the guidance of Mr. Goebel.

Mark Walker

INDEX

COSTUMES FOR EITHER MEN OR WOMEN:

MEN'S COSTUMES:

WOMEN'S COSTUMES:

COSTUMES FOR COUPLES:

GAG COSTUMES:

INTERNATIONAL COSTUMES:

BOX COSTUMES:

GOWN COSTUMES: